Getting your life to a TEN+

PRAISE for

"Kim Somers Egelsee teaches us that it is truly possible to *Live Life at a 10 Plus!* Kim has written THE guide for your life and she brilliantly shares that it's not about working harder; it's about finding your life purpose and working on yourself. When you can recognize and release the limiting beliefs that have been holding you back, anything is possible! Kim encourages her readers to seek the advice and support they need to reach the goals that they most desire. If you are ready to take your life to the next level, then get this book - and give a copy to your best friend!"

~Ursula Mentjes, Bestselling Author of
Selling with Intention

"Kim Somers Egelsee may have found the real secret to happiness. Filled with inspiration, *10 Plus* presents concrete techniques and tools to help unleash your positive power from within and conquer dreams you never would have thought possible. Lasting happiness lives within each one of us, Kim guides you to unleash the inner happiness by changing the lens through which we view daily life. A book to read time and again, bookmark, highlight and glance at whenever you need a push in the right direction."

~Amanda Russell, TV Host,
Celebrity Fitness Expert- *Hot Body Fitness*

"*10 Plus* is an insightful and refreshing read, reminding us how to unleash our authentic selves with purpose and passion. Thank you Kim, your words empower us to shine!"

~**Starla Faye**, Inspirational Speaker, Author
and *Two Talk Books* Radio Host

"Kim reveals the seven amazing steps to *Getting Your Life to a 10 Plus!* These valuable tips, intriguing exercises and doable activities will help you get clear and strong about your life purpose. Reading this book will make you feel empowered, confident and in charge of your own destiny. Living your life's purpose is achievable as Kim inspires you to have it all."

~**Susie Augustin**, Beauty Expert,
Author of *Sexy, Fit & Fab at Any Age!*

Getting your life to a TEN+

TIPS AND TOOLS FOR FINDING YOUR PURPOSE, BEING IN YOUR POWER AND LIVING AN AMAZING LIFE

Kim Somers Egelsee

GET
BRANDED
PRESS

Get Branded Press
Long Beach, CA 90803
www.getbrandedpress.com

Limits of Liability and Disclaimer of Warranty.
The author and publisher shall not be liable for your misuse of this material. This book is strictly for informational and educational purposes.

Warning – Disclaimer.
The purpose of this book is to educate and entertain. The author and/or publisher do not guarantee that anyone following these techniques, suggestions, tips, ideas, or strategies will become successful. The author and/or publisher shall have neither liability nor responsibility to anyone with respect to anyone with respect to any loss or damage caused, or alleged to be caused, directly or indirectly by the information contained in this book.

ISBN 978-0-9770018-4-2 paperback
ISBN 978-0-9770018-5-9 eBook
Library of Congress Cataloging-in-Publishing Data is available upon request.

Printed in the United States of America
First Printing, 2013

Cover Design by LivingFit OC (www.livingfitoc.com)
Interior Design by Amy Pulliam (www.creativelinc.com)
Back Cover Photography by Peter Wesley Brown

I dedicate this book to my amazing and loving husband, Edwin Egelsee, who is my best friend, love of my life, business coach, concert partner, and 100% encourager.
I am so blessed to be married to such an extraordinary man and to have two beautiful daughters together.
He truly uplifts my life in every way.

ACKNOWLEDGMENTS

I want to thank my loving family for their support: to my amazing husband, Edwin, who is also my best friend and business coach; my daughters Noella and Nia; and my parents who are super supportive and always encouraging me.

Special thanks to the following individuals: Nung Rigor who saw the inspirational speaker in me before I truly did; Susie Augustin, fabulous book editor, natural PR person, and amazing friend; Ursula Mentjes for outstanding friendship and advice; Howard Crampton Jr. for always being supportive. Arash and Therese Marquez, thank you for the great work on my CD, and to Mike Sanchez for a fantastic website and book cover. Thank you to Niurka for being a true teacher and transformational leader; Al Scaglione for being an inspiring mentor; and Joe Alexander, who first introduced my family to Jim Rohn and personal development. Mike Menjivar, I'm grateful that you saw the greatness in me when I didn't see it myself and for helping me heal through hard times. Dr. Gochette, thank you for inspiring and teaching me. Deep appreciation to all of my fellow Masterminders and friends who elevate my life constantly.

CONTENTS

Free your mind of worry about what might or might not happen, what others think of you, what you are not good at and what you did not accomplish. Focus on faith, certainty, growth, your strengths and what you love.

INTRODUCTION

The Key to Happiness, Peace and Success

Kim Somers Egelsee is an award winning inspirational speaker, author, TV host, teacher, NLP practitioner, hypnotherapist and life coach. She has a degree in Speech Communication, credentials in Educational Psychology and over 20 years of public speaking experience. She also spent over 11 years in the special education field, with an emphasis on behavior modification.

Kim specializes in helping people get every area of their lives to a 10 Plus, discover their life's purpose and be in their full positive power so that life becomes easier, happier and more fulfilling. She truly walks the walk and talks the talk, and gives you tools and tips that you can apply right away in your life. To truly love life, you need inspiration, passion, and positivity. To be "in love" with your life you need to be in your full positive power, purpose, have significance, love and relationships.

Most people have had life's circumstances such as a broken heart, a lost job, an argument, a failed exam, or even abuse that created walls around their true selves. Your heart is your true self. Imagine a photo of you. You can see your true positive powerful loving self in there, but it may have layers covering up some of the power; maybe covered with baggage through the years. The goal in working on yourself is to add positive effective pressure to shed those layers, so that your true self radiates out in full strength and confidence. Pretty soon you can see this picture of yourself without the walls and layers, and you look much brighter and very impressive.

Many of us are confused as to how to get to all of these things. Well, it all begins with a commitment to work on ourselves. Some of us get so caught up in daily life that it can become robotic and monotonous. There has to be a way to shift out of this, make some amazing changes, and move forward with enthusiasm. The good news is that there are numerous ways. Sometimes, one small shift and your entire life can change in enormous fantastic ways. So get ready…

Gold can often be found in your own backyard, gifts found in your own heart, and diamonds within your own mind.

Having a life in balance is the key to happiness, peace and success. If you can say that you have harmony in all areas of your life, it is almost 100% guaranteed that you will feel more empowered, free and happy. Extraordinary even. This means that you know your true self. You have control over your ego and you're aligned with your life purpose. To achieve this and to feel this way, start by rating everything important in your life on a scale from one to ten, everything should be rated at least a ten. This includes: relationships, social life, career or life purpose, finances, spirituality, recreational activities, health and wellness. Once you get your life to a 10, you can keep growing, and get your life to a 13 or a 20.

Getting Your Life to a 10 Plus is truly possible for anyone and everyone and so worth it. Who wouldn't want to? The **first step** is to believe it will happen. Your thoughts are more significant than you think. Focus on positive thoughts and banish all negative self-talk and beliefs. Your life can be all you can dream it to be if you believe it.

The **second step** is to make this belief a foundation by getting in alignment with your life purpose. If you're not sure what it is yet, you can state that your life purpose is to become the best you possible by getting in line with your true self. Later, you can expand on your life purpose to fit your true self precisely. How to become your best self? It does take work, but the steps are fun, amazing and become a way of life.

The **third step** is to study, learn and grow to thrive. The focus is on personal development. Begin to read inspirational books, listen to CDs in the car, watch DVDs and attend seminars. Listen to the greats; Jim Rohn, Napoleon Hill, Niurka, Anthony Robbins, John Maxwell and more. Spend at least two hours per day absorbing this life changing material. It will change your life. Your thinking will become clearer. Your thoughts will be more positive. This investment in yourself will allow you to help others just by being you.

The **fourth step** is to start evaluating your life and to identify what needs changing. Do you need to hang around more inspiring people? Do you need to stop mindless television watching? Could you spend an extra 10 minutes exercising? After making a list of these things, you can get to work. Once you make the space by getting rid of anything negative, you make room for greatness to come in.

The **fifth step** is to seek those who can help you get to that next level of joy and success with positive influence, advice and guidance. Be around like-minded positive people and form or join a mastermind group. Everyone can benefit from a mentor or coach. Almost no one can do it alone. This coach or mentor can help you with setting and achieving goals, releasing emotional baggage, guidance, and working on aspects of your life that could use improvement such as finances, relationships or purpose in life.

The **sixth step** is goal setting. Think big and dare to dream. It's best to pick about three goals to start with. Make sure that they are in line with your true self and to word them positively. Break these goals into benchmarks, and take steps daily towards these goals.

The **seventh** and most important step is value. Check yourself regularly by asking questions and taking action. Evaluate by asking yourself if the way you are acting, behaving, talking and being who you truly are is in line with your purpose. Make sure that what you are regularly reading, where you are going, who you are with, and what you are doing are matching that of which you see yourself becoming. Be sure that you are taking action daily on getting your life to this high level of happiness and success, and soon you will realize that you have reached a **10 PLUS Life.**

Getting your life
to a TEN+

CHAPTER ONE

THERE IS POWER IN BELIEVING YOU CAN

Turtles, clams and snails are meant to have shells. Humans are not. Take yours off and dare to let your true self out to shine.

STEP 1

The first step in *Getting Your Life to a 10 Plus* is to believe you can. If you don't believe in yourself and your capabilities, it cannot happen. The way that this can occur is to change the way that you talk to yourself and evaluate your current beliefs. Make sure there is no negative self talk. Instead of telling yourself that you are not good enough, this can never happen, that you'd do that if only; start telling yourself that you are incredible, that you can and will do it! It's extraordinary how a few words have the power to change people's lives.

Language is amazing, and the way you use it when you talk to yourself and others can affect your mood, behavior, personality and overall life choices. Getting into the habit of thinking and speaking positively will change your life in astounding ways. Even if you don't consciously believe it at first, you can train your brain to think so, and then know so.

It is very common for people to have continuous negative thoughts popping into their heads throughout the day. Limiting beliefs such as "I'm not good enough", "I might fail at this", or "I'm scared that I will not make enough money" may also come to mind. Some people may feel like they have a continuous chorus of negativity flying around up there.

What you have to do is train your brain to stop this chatter. It is possible to do this. You have control. Get into rapport with yourself. First, stop watching negative news or television, reading unconstructive books or magazines, and attending low energy events. This becomes ingrained into your consciousness and adds to the negative chorus in your mind.

Next, stop hanging around anyone who is too pessimistic or brings you down. You know those people who continuously talk about how bad everything is; blaming the world for their lives. These are the people whose energy will rub off on you and affect your life. Hanging around negative people can nudge you daily off course. The cumulative effect of this over five or ten years could have a significant impact on your life. There is a big difference between someone who truly wants help and advice, and one who attracts and gives out drama. You don't have time for them.

Now you are ready to train your brain. Each time you start

to have a disempowering word, thought or belief come up that you know is not true, think of a specific spot in the ocean, and imagine throwing the thought out to sea. The saltwater will dissolve the negativity, and the more that you do this, little by little, you will have less negative beliefs scattering around up there.

Another effective technique is to step aside, look in and laugh at the thoughts that come up, because deep inside you know that they are not the true you. The more often that you can look in and laugh at them, knowing they are not who you really are, you give them less power. They begin to go away. Your true self is love. You are powerful. So when those unwanted negative thoughts and feelings appear, make sure that you remind yourself that they aren't real.

For example, Maria constantly gets thoughts popping into her mind about being stupid, not good enough and lazy. She is actually a successful realtor and an extreme go-getter. These thoughts used to hold her back from taking bigger actions. After using this technique, Maria began laughing at these false thoughts, and reminded herself that she is great and powerful. Thus, she began taking larger risks and actions in her life and career.

It's important to start being aware of when you think or say that you "ought to", "should", or "must do" something. This means that you believe that you are obligated to do it, that it's your duty or requirement. Next, make sure that the things that you do believe are really about you. These may be comments or criticisms that you were told at a young age that have stuck with you. Sometimes it's difficult for people to let go of words and beliefs if they came from a loved one. It stems from a fear of that parent figure or loved one no longer being right, and not being a hero anymore. It's okay to realize that these people were wrong about you.

Make a list of the things you are angry at or blaming people for. Sit with your list for a day. Come up with positive opposites to find ways to forgive, such as, they did the best they knew how at the time. Then, let it go, and know that they did their best with the tools that they had, just like you are doing.

Fortunately these beliefs can all be changed. The tools can all be learned. Start today with evaluating the words you use and the beliefs that you have about yourself. Do you remember the childhood saying "sticks and stones may break my bones, but words can never hurt me"? This is not true. Words are very powerful, and can even have a physiological and psychological effect.

Turn anything that is negative into a positive and watch your life change as you start to soar. You may be saying to yourself at this point that it is easier said than done. It really isn't. It's simply a daily commitment to retrain your mind on how to think. You have one life on this earth. It takes the same amount of energy to have a negative and insignificant life. Why not make it a successful, fulfilled, significant life? You have the power.

Most people feel in some form that they are not good enough. We are not born with most of our beliefs. Our beliefs are learned and made up throughout childhood experiences, what others have told us, things that we have experienced or encountered, and sometimes through our culture. The humorous part is that if everyone feels this way, we can laugh it off , not take ourselves too seriously, and just be who we truly are. Our new belief can be, "I am approved, accepted and complete." Even if you are working on yourself, you are the best you for today.

An example of this is Hillary, who believes that if she leaves the house in the morning with the bed unmade and the dishes not done, she is a bad wife and mother. She is very hard on herself. She has formed the belief throughout her life, most likely stemming from something she learned in childhood, that if you don't get all of the chores done, you're not good enough. Fortunately, it's just all a story that Hillary has been telling herself all of her life. It's time to change the story to, "I am a great and empowered wife regardless, and I am doing the best I can. Whether the chores are done or not does not define who I am!"

On another note, some of us have been raised to believe that "money is the root of all evil." A powerful phrase to repeat to yourself is "money is the root of all miracles." It is. Think about it. Money, when used wisely, can do spectacular things for you, your family and others. For some crazy reason, most of us grew up with the "evil" belief, but that's just not true. This new attitude that you create about money being a miracle will remove blocks in your financial flow, creating new opportunities for abundance to come soaring through to you.

Mark was brought up with money issues. He has been a bartender for years in a small restaurant in New York City. He makes decent money to stay afloat in his life with his one bedroom rental apartment. He dreams of owning a home one day and being more financially stable. One day, Mark gets a job offer to bartend in a fancy hotel nearby where he would triple his earnings. He turns down the job offer; he believes that he wouldn't fit in, people wouldn't tip him well, and he wouldn't be able to handle the pressure of working in a luxury hotel. Mark just turned down an offer to live more comfortably, have the means to help others, and even save enough money to buy himself a home. Mark is living by his beliefs that he has decided are true. He believes that he is not good enough, and that money is the root of all evil. If Mark wants to move forward in his life, he could take the new job and save for a home. He could challenge himself to be even greater and have pride in his own abilities, realizing that money can be used for beautiful things.

Even if you initially do not believe the things you are telling yourself, your mind will absorb it, and eventually believe it. I know this sounds a bit odd, but think about it. You have believed you are not good enough only because you have chosen to believe this story. Turn it around! Tell yourself a new story; that you are powerful, strong and undefeatable. This will result in enormous positive changes and opportunities in your life. The first step is to believe you can get your life to a 10 Plus. If you don't believe in yourself and your capabilities, it cannot happen.

You have the power to decide if you want to be happy or sad, elated or mad, enthusiastic or deflated. What do you decide? Remember, it takes the same amount of energy, so why not choose happy, elated and enthusiastic?

CHAPTER ONE: TIPS AND TOOLS

1. Believe.
2. Turn negative self-talk into positive thinking.
3. Stop watching the news, hanging out with pessimistic people, and making negative choices.
4. Throw the disempowering thoughts out into the ocean or laugh at them, knowing they are not the real you.
5. Be aware of your beliefs and thoughts.
6. Start evaluating where your beliefs came from. Are they really true?
7. Change your old disempowering beliefs into new empowering ones.
8. Make a list of the friends that SUE you; Support, Uplift and Encourage you.

TIPS AND TOOLS

_____

_____

_____

_____

_____

_____

_____

_____

_____

_____

_____

_____

_____

_____

_____

_____

_____

_____

_____

_____

_____

_____

EXERCISE

Take five minutes to list any negative thoughts or beliefs that regularly come up for you. Now evaluate where they came from and learn from them. How have they worked for your life? Next to each one, create a constructive encouraging thought or belief that you will adopt. Then, list what it will cost you in your life if you were to hold on to that negative thought or belief. How will your life change for the better if you were to rid yourself of these thoughts and beliefs?

EXERCISE

_____

_____

_____

_____

_____

_____

_____

_____

_____

_____

_____

_____

_____

_____

_____

_____

_____

_____

_____

_____

_____

_____

_____

How to Overcome Obstacles, Grief and Difficulties to Get to Success "Triumph Over Tragedy"

1. Feel it, so that it doesn't get repressed.
2. Don't remain stuck in the problem as the victim, filled with guilt.
3. Find the gift.
4. Step back and analyze, get curious, ask "why me?"
5. Realize that even a few minutes ago you didn't know how to handle it as well as you do now.
6. Read books on healing.
7. Talk to positive people or get a support system.
8. Pray, meditate and visualize.
9. Focus on 5 things that you are grateful for.
10. Move forward to new opportunities and keep going.
11. Embrace meaningful activities of giving.
12. Believe you will succeed, expect it.
13. Laugh and play, embrace your inner child, and do things that used to make you happy.
14. Celebrate the strength, non-judgment, wisdom and courage you have developed.
15. Face your challenges, inadequacies, weaknesses or mistakes and change them; are you willing?
16. What are you focusing on?
17. Celebrate what you are good at, the good you have done for others and great things that have happened.
18. Realize you are not the only one; this is part of your growth, life and experience.

Write down the tools that you will use. Which ones resonate with you, help you and will encourage you?

_____

_____

_____

_____

_____

_____

_____

_____

_____

_____

_____

_____

_____

_____

_____

_____

_____

_____

_____

_____

_____

_____

Getting your life
to a **TEN+**

CHAPTER TWO

DISCOVERING YOUR LIFE PURPOSE

*Create your own SPECTACULAR opportunities
and jump into them.*

STEP 2

The second step in *Getting Your Life to a 10 Plus* is to know your life purpose. If you don't know your life's purpose, you can make your purpose, "I will be the best me I can possibly be." This means dedicating time to working on you. Doing this will reap considerable benefits and begin pulling you towards positivity, success, wealth and great relationships.

When you truly get aligned with your life purpose you can look back and say, "Ah, now I know why those other things in my life didn't seem to work." In reality they worked out exactly as they were meant to be, perfectly so your purpose could be found. From these events, occurrences and happenings you have learned, grown and expanded as a person. You are closer to what you want, and may be clear about what you don't want. For example, I had always thought that my life purpose lay in the entertainment industry. I spent years pursuing acting, modeling and producing. I did extra work, landed bit parts, joined Screen Actors Guild, I sang in a rock group and more. Although I truly enjoyed it, I felt a bit of a strain. Something was missing and I did not feel complete. In addition, I had also worked in the field of special education; both with adults with disabilities and severe behavior issues, as well as with children with moderate to severe disabilities, mainly in wheelchairs. While I loved it, I was still yearning for something more.

I worked on myself spiritually and prayed for my perfect self expression to be found. I let go of disempowering beliefs and layers of baggage. My life purpose found me and I stepped into it. I now feel 100% whole, complete, purposeful, on fire, and so excited about it all. My life purpose is to teach others to lead an extraordinary life through life coaching, inspirational speaking and leading by example. All of this while empowering myself, my family and others to be happy, joyful and close to God. I do this through speaking at numerous events and workshops, co- hosting an inspiring TV show, contributing to multiple magazines, coaching others and much more.

Throughout our lives we achieve, succeed, learn, grow and play. We do much of this with the help, participation and involvement of other people. Sometimes we have a group of people that we spend regular time with. Other times it's our best friend, significant other or co-worker. Additionally, it can be the help of a mentor, coach, workshop or seminar. One phrase or sentence from someone can be life-changing, inspirational and filled with meaning. Something you hear, learn or experience can cause you to change your path and move toward your true dreams. Regardless of which person is involved, we get a lot of joy from letting others into our lives. Relationships are fundamental to a fulfilling life.

Following your passion makes life easier, more fulfilling and enables you to be a living example. For some people in today's times, a new business or a side business can lead to greater income, freedom and stability. For others, moving up or growing in their current career is inspirational. Ultimately, finding your deep dreams, passions and purpose is the key to getting every area of your life to a 10 Plus.

Desire used in a positive way is the key to getting what you want in life; it will help you find your purpose, or let your purpose find you. Desire is having a mixture of hope, faith and eagerness related to where you see yourself, who you see yourself with, and what you see yourself doing in life. It is a strong motive mixed with passion, inspiration, intention and action. Desires, when used in a powerful manner, always mixed with a good amount of reason, can get a person to create their own opportunities and jump into them, buy the home they've always dreamed of, find their life's purpose, be with their true soul mate, and more. Desire begins as a thought, is then mixed with passion and inspiration, and with hope and faith, it turns into motivated action. I have found that when the desire is strong enough, how you accomplish your goals becomes easier.

An important aspect of your life to assess is to ask if there is anything unnecessary or negative present that needs modification or elimination. Are you spending time with draining people or are you in a job that you don't enjoy? Are you watching too much television or playing video games daily? Make a list of at least three things that you can lessen or get rid of to make room for true desire to come in and uplift your life. When this space is created it leaves your mind open and the desires can begin. There is room to realize that maybe you'd like more positive people in your life, some extra date nights with your partner, or a dream career.

There is now room for your brain to start working. This making space is so profound that sometimes you are just led into opportunities through your new, stronger intuition. For example, being guided to those who could teach you the information that could help you begin that dream job, meeting the right new people, and more.

EXERCISE

To help you find your purpose, or to make sure your current purpose is really your true calling, think of everything that makes you feel fulfilled in your life. Then, think of five words or values to describe these things. For example, if someone is fulfilled by their family life and their career, their five words or values describing these two aspects might be integrity, love, patience, passion and motivation. These powerful words can help them with their life purpose, to make sure it is aligned with the words that describe what is essential for them.

Now, take out a sheet of paper and title it, "What does my truest self want?" Underneath the title write a free flowing of all that comes out of your pen without consciously thinking about it for five minutes. Just let it flow. This means write out every dream, whether you think the dream is realistic or not.

Look over your list and circle the items that can be described with your five essential words. This will give you clarity. It will help you see which of your items is truly aligned with what is fulfilling and important to you. Your purpose may still take some time, but this will help you to focus on what is meaningful. It will eliminate that which doesn't match your words of essence.

Finally, write out your life purpose in a few sentences and carry it with you everywhere. Review your purpose frequently so that it's in your mind. This way, for all that you do, you can ask yourself if it is in line with your true calling. It's okay if you modify it over time. The important thing is to move forward with the intention of knowing your true self and purpose in life. This is a huge step in *Getting Your Life to a 10 Plus*. You will have this in your mind at all times. Your life purpose will guide you in how you make all your decisions; what to do, what to say, and who to spend time with. You will be able to stop and ask yourself if going to an event, hanging out with a particular person, or choosing a new venture is aligned with your life purpose. If not, you can say no. Now everything will be easier.

EXERCISE

_____

_____

_____

_____

_____

_____

_____

_____

_____

_____

_____

_____

_____

_____

_____

_____

_____

_____

_____

_____

_____

_____

CHAPTER 2: TIPS AND TOOLS

1. Be the best "you" you can be. Study and work on yourself.
2. Let go of disempowering thoughts and beliefs.
3. Pray or declare that you will find your perfect self-expression.
4. Think of what makes you feel grateful or fulfilled in your life.
5. Write down the words, adjectives or emotions that describe these things.

   (Ex: passionate, inspired, calm, etc.)
6. Take 5 minutes to write the answers to "What does my truest self really want?" Now circle those that stand out, and match your values and essential words.
7. You are now at or closer to your true life purpose.

THE LIFE PURPOSE FORMULA

Life Purpose + Intention + Positive Words,
People and Action + What You Radiate + Let Go
= It Will Flow

Your purpose mixed with each intention you have, can be powerfully combined with positive people around you, positive thoughts and communication, and forward action. Next, you radiate out what you want to receive back. Now, you have done it all, so let go without fear of failing, and everything will flow how it is meant to.

EXERCISE

1. Make a list of all of the talents and things you were good at from ages four through the present.
2. Notice what stands out to you that could translate into your purpose today.
3. Circle the things that stand out to you.
4. Make a list of what you are grateful for.
5. Write out your life purpose in a few sentences and carry it with you everywhere, reviewing it daily.

EXERCISE

_____

_____

_____

_____

_____

_____

_____

_____

_____

_____

_____

_____

_____

_____

_____

_____

_____

_____

_____

_____

_____

MY LIFE PURPOSE STATEMENT

(Be sure to add "you" in your statement!)

_____

_____

_____

_____

_____

_____

_____

_____

_____

_____

_____

_____

_____

_____

_____

_____

_____

_____

_____

_____

_____

_____

_____

_____

Getting your life
to a **TEN+**

CHAPTER THREE

STUDY, LEARN AND GROW TO THRIVE

Know + Grow + Show = Glow
The more you know, the greater you will grow, which shows
through your radiating glow that attracts people and
opportunities to you.

STEP 3

The third step in *Getting Your Life to a 10 Plus* is to study, learn and grow. Spend at least two hours per day with personal development. Listen to CDs while driving, watch inspirational DVDs, attend motivational/inspirational seminars regularly, talk to amazing people, ask lots of questions, and read at least one book per month. There is so much wonderful information out there that can truly change your life. Spend time with the greats; Chris Widener, Og Mandino, John Maxwell, Jim Rohn, SUCCESS Magazine, Niurka, Dr. Wayne Dyer, Ursula Mentjes, Napoleon Hill, Florence Scovel Shinn, Shajen Joy Aziz, Doreen Virtue, Joel Osteen, Anthony Robbins, Starla Porter, W. Clement Stone, Marianne Williamson, and more.

One of the fastest ways for you to grow yourself and your

business, find your purpose, meet phenomenal people, gain life-altering knowledge, evolve as a person, and have the positive powerful energy of success is to be involved in a mastermind and/or regularly attend workshops, seminars, events or retreats.

Many wonder what all of the fuss or hype is all about. Why can't I just sit home and read or watch a DVD? Reading, watching a DVD, or listening to inspiring CDs in the car are very effective ways to grow and achieve. However, the difference when you actually attend and participate in a positive live event or meeting is huge. You truly stimulate all of your senses and engage your mind in very deep ways. The energy created by you and those around you can be felt throughout the room. The energy of being involved in a mastermind, workshop, seminar or retreat with positive people creating growth and change together is an extraordinary shift for all involved. However, you do have to be involved.

Tips for Getting the Most Out of Seminars and Retreats

1. Choose the right ones to attend with your heart and your intuition. Ask empowering questions; are the right positive like-minded people going to attend? Does this topic stimulate my mind? Would my life be enhanced by attending this? Would memories be created by being there?

2. Have the intention right away that you will grow and evolve. Soak it in. It doesn't mean that you have to use all of the information, but take it in like a college course, and use what applies to you.

3. Communicate with others there; the attendees, the speaker or teacher. Get to know them. Some of the people you meet at seminars become life-long friends, strategic partners, referral buddies, accountability partners and more. I have personally done the research. Personal development events are the best way to meet the people that uplift you and help you in your success in business.

4. Take notes, visualize, be receptive and open-minded. Take it in and apply it.

5. Participate. Play full out!

6. Be approachable and flexible.

7. Feel the energy, power, greatness of knowledge and extraordinary learning, growth and change.

8.   Finally, realize that when you step out of your home or office, into an event or workshop that inspires, it brings out your spirit within, as there are no phone calls, computers, or distractions nearby. It elevates your consciousness bit by bit. And, step by step you evolve into your true self.

Try it! Try this for one month, and see how your life changes and moves forward. Your thinking will become clearer, you will focus more, and the secrets to success and happiness will become your essence, a part of you, until you just exude it and it is you.

CHAPTER THREE: TIPS AND TOOLS

1. Realize that there is growth and learning in every experience and encounter, whether you choose to label it good or bad. Get in the habit of looking for it, finding it, and applying it.
2. Subscribe to a great inspirational monthly magazine such as *Today's Innovative Woman, Inspirational Woman,* or *SUCCESS Magazine.*
3. Attend personal development seminars. This is where you will learn, grow, and make amazing connections with people who can become your life-long friends and referral partners.
4. Take notes on what you learn, read and listen to.
5. Ask questions.
6. Get a new certification or degree.

EXERCISE

Write down how much time you currently spend on working on yourself. Now, write down in what ways you are studying, learning and growing. How has this already changed your life, and how do you think it will in the future? How would your life be impacted if you did not work on yourself?

EXERCISE

_____

_____

_____

_____

_____

_____

_____

_____

_____

_____

_____

_____

_____

_____

_____

_____

_____

_____

_____

_____

_____

_____

_____

_____

CHAPTER FOUR

EVALUATE AND APPRAISE YOURSELF
YOU ARE WORTH IT

Get into the habit of stepping aside and observing yourself
regularly for extra power.

STEP 4

The fourth step in *Getting Your Life to a 10 Plus* involves regular evaluation and appraisal of yourself. I suggest you truly look at what you are regularly doing at least four times per year. Assess and analyze the following questions: Who are you spending your time with? Are you meeting your goals? What in your life is going great? What improvements are needed? How do you feel overall on a daily basis?

Review for a few minutes at the end of each day, an hour at the end of each week, a few hours at the end of each month, and a day or so at the end of the year. This can involve a retreat or simply an hour of your time in a quiet area with a blank sheet of paper or your journal.

Write out everything and analyze it. A retreat can be defined as an hour out of the day where you take your dog for a walk, a day with friends at an event, a weekend in San Diego, or a full vacation in Hawaii. Whatever you decide, it's important to realize that this is needed. You may be saying that you don't have the time or cannot afford to do all of this reflection. However, please be advised that you cannot afford not to reflect on your life frequently and check in on how you are doing. So many people stagger through their lives without doing any constructive thinking. Then, unfortunately, they reach retirement age and ask: "Where did my life go? What did I accomplish? What am I going to do now? Did I live out what I truly wanted?" The saddest thing is to live your life without purpose or meaning. This is the difference between making a living and designing a life! I beg you to seek to design your life.

Retreats revitalize you, creating vibrancy, joy, calmness, clarity and warmth in your life. This leads to you looking at life in a positive way and living balanced. It's a way to begin *Getting Your Life to a 10 Plus.* Time away from your home, bills, career and everyday activities helps you see what you have done well to celebrate successes, and fuels you to move forward toward your dreams. Time spent away in retreat can quiet your mind, keeping it open to new ideas and for opportunities to enter. Most importantly, a walk, a mini trip, a seminar or a vacation energize you to be better in all you do.

An additional suggestion is to meet with someone on a weekly basis to talk about and evaluate your life and your goals. For example, on Sunday evenings my husband and

I take an hour at dinner to discuss our week. We talk about the amazing things we did, what we learned, how we can get better, and the steps we took toward our goals. These dinners are often celebrations of our successes that week. They also consist of honest feedback and suggestions. We even involve our young daughter Noella.

A thorough way to self-evaluate and grow is with the help of a life coach or mentor. Meet with the person regularly to review your life. This enables you to make profound, meaningful changes and move forward. A mastermind group is also fun and great for accountability. It is a group of like-minded people you meet with once or twice per month to network, discuss goals and receive ideas, inspiring you to follow through with your dreams. This powerful team of success-minded beings becomes one another's support system.

Remember to ask yourself the following questions on a regular basis in order to evaluate that you are moving forward in life:

Who am I spending time with?
What am I doing with my time?
What choices am I making?
What can I do to be more successful, happier and more fulfilled?
If I say yes to this, what am I saying no to?

Most importantly, be proud of yourself. Just the time you take to learn how you are doing is a step in the right direction.

_____

_____

_____

_____

_____

_____

_____

_____

_____

_____

_____

_____

_____

_____

_____

_____

_____

_____

_____

CHAPTER FOUR: TIPS AND TOOLS

1. Regularly evaluate each area of your life; ten being amazing and exceptional, and zero being terrible.
2. Choose a person or group to regularly meet with for encouragement, accountability and success.
3. Become aware of the daily steps you are taking at all times, making sure it is aligned with your purpose or essence.
4. Celebrate successes and steps toward greatness. Know yourself, read, study, attend seminars, work with a coach or mentor, and spend time with like-minded positive people.
5. Find out and know your life purpose, what makes you energized and fulfilled.
6. Purpose + Intention + Positive People + Thoughts and Actions + What you Radiate + Let Go
   = It will Flow.
7. Be happy and remind your brain when you are happy; it trains you to look for and embrace happiness more often.
8. Be in your full positive power.
9. Create your own power phrase (Example: My smile exudes joy, passion and inspiration!)
10. Ask 5 people you trust to give you feedback.
11. Laugh at yourself more.
12. Live by example; you can change someone's life with a sentence.
13. Keep photos of you at your best.
14. Look into the mirror until you love yourself.

15. Practice affirmations daily.
16. See beauty in everything.
17. Meditate, pray, be in nature, garden, paint or sing.

TIPS AND TOOLS

_____

_____

_____

_____

_____

_____

_____

_____

_____

_____

_____

_____

_____

_____

_____

_____

_____

_____

_____

_____

_____

_____

EXERCISE

Create a bucket list of dreams, goals and items you want to achieve in the next year. Ask yourself if you followed your heart, what would make you not just happy or content but truly fulfilled. Think big, and really see yourself achieving these things. Now rewrite it onto a nice sheet of linen, and tape it onto your mirror or wall to be viewed daily. Create a dream board of these visions, with pictures that you adore from magazines, onto a poster board of your ideal size.

EXERCISE

_____

_____

_____

_____

_____

_____

_____

_____

_____

_____

_____

_____

_____

_____

_____

_____

_____

_____

_____

_____

_____

_____

_____

EXERCISE

_____

_____

_____

_____

_____

_____

_____

_____

_____

_____

_____

_____

_____

_____

_____

_____

_____

_____

_____

_____

_____

_____

10 Tips and Tools for What's Important in Leadership, Success and Prosperity

1. Lead yourself; focus, be clear, motivate and inspire yourself to move forward with purpose, intention, passion and action. Live by example.
2. Position yourself as an expert. If you don't believe in you, no one else can. Have confidence. Play Big, Bigger, Biggest!
3. Walk the walk and talk the talk; having been there, done that, doing it, living it.
4. Reminder: Bad thoughts= toxins to you and others; Good thoughts= fuel for self and others.
5. Truly realize that you can learn from everyone. Have genuine appreciation. No hierarchy.
6. Focus on the positive. No blaming (think where the person is coming from, good or evil).
7. Develop ideas, effectively plan, implement them with action and teamwork, and receive feedback and results.
8. Inspiration + Preparation + Engagement of a group or organization to achieve.
9. Stand out by being your true self, being bold, and being outspoken in a positive way.
10. Balance your schedule. Leave time for you. Don't do too many things at once.

Getting your life
to a **TEN+**

CHAPTER FIVE

ADVICE, GUIDANCE AND
ENCOURAGEMENT

*The power of great advice, guidance and wisdom
can accelerate success.*

STEP 5

The fifth step in *Getting Your Life to a 10 Plus* is to seek advice and guidance. Asking for help can sometimes be difficult. We may feel that in doing so, we are being weak or even silly. However, everyone can use help, mentoring, coaching or advice in their lives. Relationships are what keep our lives vibrant, joyful and fun!

Great thinkers and wealth builders of the world got to where they were with the help of others, their families and their mastermind groups. You should feel strong every time you ask for advice or guidance, as these are steps to bettering yourself. The growth and knowledge you gain are invaluable. You will be able to move forward fearlessly in taking daily steps to greatness.

People need one another. Relationships are the beauty of life. To truly see themselves clearer and more objectively, most people need support of some sort. It may be in the form of a coach, mentor, best friend, or counselor. A mastermind group is also a great support for motivation, inspiration and accountability. If you can say that your life is not at a 10 in all areas you can use some help. Evaluate your spiritual life, self care, social life, love relationship, friendships, family life, career, life purpose and finances. Even the people whose lives are at a 10 Plus, regularly get advice and guidance from someone.

Accepting help, kindness and generosity from friends and loved ones is an exceptional thing. It makes you feel loved and supported, and the other person feels wonderful as well. The important thing is to use this assistance as a growth experience. Why not create your life by design and let yourself soar? What would that be worth to you? Do you believe that it's possible? Of course it is!

It's also important to remember that it's about collaboration and not competition. Everyone is unique. There is room in this world for all to achieve and succeed. Even when someone sells the same product or teaches the same subject, we all have our own spice to add to it that will meet the needs of the right people for us. Take a look at some of the world's most successful people; Oprah Winfrey, Donald Trump, Tony Robbins and more. They all have a team! Any success is a collaborative effort, not the result of a single person.

Now that you have made the conscious decision to have an extraordinary life, what do you do? Who do you contact? Take some time to think about who would be your best fit. Would a life coach help you get to the next level and eliminate negativity? Do you need a mentor, someone that you can regularly meet with and learn from? Would you benefit from going to five great seminars this year? Perhaps you should join a mastermind group, or form your own.

All of the above would be ideal. Why not push your own envelope and move quickly toward greatness this year? Think on it, plan it, and take action!

CHAPTER FIVE: TIPS AND TOOLS

1. Ask for help.
2. Collaboration, not competition.
3. When you ask for help, feel strong.
4. Join a mastermind or networking group, or meet with a positive group regularly.

EXERCISE

Make a list of who supports and uplifts you today. Who could you ask help from? List 10 people that you would like to connect with to help you create an extraordinary life. Where can you go to connect with them? How often will you meet with someone?

EXERCISE

_____

_____

_____

_____

_____

_____

_____

_____

_____

_____

_____

_____

_____

_____

_____

_____

_____

_____

_____

_____

_____

_____

EXERCISE

_____

_____

_____

_____

_____

_____

_____

_____

_____

_____

_____

_____

_____

_____

_____

_____

_____

_____

_____

_____

_____

_____

Getting your life
to a TEN+

CHAPTER SIX

GOALS TO GREATNESS, ABUNDANCE AND A SPECTACULAR LIFE

GOALS: Gain Outstanding Achievement through Love and Success.

Step 6

The sixth step in *Getting Your Life to a 10 Plus* is setting goals to greatness. This step is significant in getting your life balanced, tranquil and amazing. Goals are a way for you to gain outstanding achievement through love and success. This means that for each of your goals, get to whatever outstanding achievement means to you in your heart. Mix this with love and taking action toward a desired outcome. This is a positive formula for meeting your goals. It is best to pick three goals, with one of them being the biggest and most emphasized. Make sure that these goals are in line with your life purpose. As you get comfortable and motivated with taking the steps toward these goals, you can add more.

Create a list of your goals and dreams. Spend several minutes thinking about what you are grateful for and what you feel could make you even happier. Think about what you enjoy doing so much that it is effortless, as well as what you loved doing as a child.

After creating this list, evaluate how each of these goals makes you feel and if they truly fit the real you. Does being grateful for family make you feel joyful? If you would be happier in a different career would that give you an enthusiastic feeling? As a child, did playing softball make you feel free? If yes, then your special feelings would be joy, enthusiasm, and freedom. These will help you in deciding if your goals meet your true conscious needs. It's helpful to know that the most common regret of those dying was that they did not live for themselves, and instead lived for what they thought others wanted of them.

An example of goal setting is Joe's goal is to become more organized at work by the end of the year. Joe realizes that he needs a goal that makes him feel appreciated, calm and focused. By creating this goal of organization, the outcome should give him these three feelings. On the other hand, Joe has another goal to begin playing in a local band on the weekends by November. He evaluated this, and realized that this goal's outcome or result would not make him feel calm or focused. Therefore, he eliminated that goal, and chooses to jam with friends once in awhile instead.

Be sure that each of your goals has benchmarks or steps for achievement. For example: by June of this year, I will have my closets completely organized so that my life is more efficient. By the end of the year, I will have fifty new positive business contacts that I met through networking groups, workshops and events. What will you do each week to ensure that this goal is met?

It is helpful to find an accountability partner to keep you on track. It also works well to mark these steps into your planner each week. You can post your purpose and goals in an area of your home, where you are continuously reminded of what you are working towards. Additionally, it is an excellent idea to write out your purpose and goals on an index card to keep in your purse, cell phone or wallet. You can add affirmations or tips for living well too. This way you will stay on track by constantly being reminded of your greatness. Goals ensure that you are moving forward.

CHAPTER SIX: TIPS AND TOOLS

1. Your goals should meet your personal definition of outstanding achievement.
2. Your goals can match your life's purpose, or be in line with personal growth, healing or development.
3. Make sure each goal is positive and will help you move forward.
4. Be sure that each goal makes you feel good, and excited for taking action.

EXERCISE

Think about what makes you feel motivated, excited or inspired. Now think about what goals would meet your purpose, path or personal growth. Spend ten minutes writing what comes to you. Now take a minute and circle the top three. Make sure each goal is worded in the positive. For example, "By May of this year I will run the 5 mile marathon with grace and ease, to be fit, healthy and disciplined." Write these three goals now.

EXERCISE

_____

_____

_____

_____

_____

_____

_____

_____

_____

_____

_____

_____

_____

_____

_____

_____

_____

_____

_____

_____

_____

_____

EXERCISE

_____

_____

_____

_____

_____

_____

_____

_____

_____

_____

_____

_____

_____

_____

_____

_____

_____

_____

_____

_____

_____

_____

_____

Getting your life to a **TEN+**

CHAPTER SEVEN

VALUE IS YOUR FORTUNE

Ask yourself if you would do business with yourself, if you would spend time with yourself, and if you would be your friend.

Step 7

The seventh and final step in *Getting Your Life to a 10 Plus* is to find out the value and integrity of what you are doing. Where are you going and who you are spending time with? What you are saying to yourself and others? Do you walk your talk? Do you value yourself and others?

Take some time each month to ask yourself where you are at in all areas of your life. How are your relationships, social life, career, life purpose, spirituality, fun and recreation, finances, health and wellness? Rate yourself.

There may be some areas where you are not at a high level yet. Find out why. What choices could you make to raise this rating? Can you get rid of some things in your life in order to focus on what is of true value to you? Do whatever you can to move forward. Ask for help, read books and take steps toward greatness. It is so worth it!

A typical day for someone can include going to the gym, working all day, making phone calls and sending emails, eating healthy as well as fitting in some social, quiet and family time. Sometimes we have so much to do it becomes overwhelming. The first thing to do is to eliminate the word "overwhelmed" from your vocabulary, and begin to say that you are "in demand". This is an empowering word that implies that you are needed and what you do daily does make a difference in the world.

It's a good idea to have a planner where you write down your benchmarks, objectives or projects for each day. Be sure to break them into realistic steps. Too much crammed into one day can lead to feeling burned out. Each week make a list of all that you want to do, and assign dates for each item. Regularly check back with your planner to make sure that you are on top of your game. It helps to place stars or check marks where you've accomplished things. It's also very helpful to have an accountability partner who you can regularly talk to about what you are getting done and achieving. This keeps you on track and focused on your goals.

CHAPTER SEVEN: TIPS AND TOOLS

1. Find out the value of what you are doing. Do you regard yourself highly? Does it show? Are you fair to yourself?
2. Evaluate the areas of your life from one to ten every few months.
3. Spend time on areas that you need to improve.
4. Ask others for feedback.
5. Evaluate your inner feelings, energy and vibes. Use your intuition more.

EXERCISE

Think about the value you are giving out every day. Are you radiating out to the world what you want to get in return? Are you walking the walk and talking the talk? Do you have high self-appreciation and acceptance? Does it show? If you answered no to any of these, what do you feel is missing? What can you do to improve? Who can you ask for feedback or help with this?

EXERCISE

_____

_____

_____

_____

_____

_____

_____

_____

_____

_____

_____

_____

_____

_____

_____

_____

_____

_____

_____

_____

_____

_____

_____

_____

Getting your life
to a **TEN**✚

BONUS CHAPTER

HOW TO BE IN YOUR FULL POSITIVE POWER:
Fear is Denying Yourself the Permission to Have it All

An amazing way to live is by feeling 100% confident in your full positive power. This means being in love with yourself, feeling confidence in any interaction, applauding yourself for your achievements, exuding and radiating joy, being excited about life, and having the nerve to be YOU. Having the vulnerability to be open, accessible to others, and living by example.

Being in your full power means being an example by just being you. Your energy is so strong and positive that people and opportunities are drawn to you naturally. Your life's purpose becomes clearer and you are more focused. You dare to smile at strangers, speak up at events or meetings, take steps daily toward your dreams, and dance around when you feel like it. What a fun and adventurous way to live!

Think of people that are in their full power. They are all uplifting the world with their unique personalities and you can too! These human beings all have extreme confidence, are daring, bold, outspoken, know their purpose, and play hard. They make sure to truly take large and small steps toward their passions each day. These steps accumulate into epic extraordinary life experiences. Even if it isn't your thing to be noticed, you can be in your full positive power, quietly radiating it out to the world, happier than you have ever been.

Start by creating a journal for two weeks and write down how you were in your full power each day. You will be more aware of your behaviors, communication, attitude and self daily, which will motivate you to go for it. Learn from others, books, workshops and practice. You will begin waking up excited to start each day, embracing new opportunities and life overall.

Power is Having Capability, Effectiveness, Talents, Potential and Dynamism

How do you begin to utilize your full positive power? Remember the acronym PASSION.

P Live with **P**assion
A Take **A**ction with a positive **A**ttitude
S Exude **S**pirit and **S**punk
S Be **S**avvy
I   Embrace and use your **I**ntelligence/smarts;
      Intuition/gather the knowledge
O Be **O**pen minded/**O**utspoken
N Have the **N**erve to be yourself

If you want to do something out of your usual comfort zone that you know would elevate your life, think of it as an exciting thrill ride, a trip to a new land, a chance to be a new and better you. Go for it. Take action. Stand out from the crowd.

PASSION

We all have an inner scale that points to yes or no; or high energy or low energy. When we are doing something we love, spending time with positive people or having a great experience, your inner scale is weighing to the positive. If we are with negative influences, in a job we dislike, or at an event that doesn't float our boat, our inner scale will tilt to the low energy scale. The key is to notice when we get the positive yes scale to the tippy top where we feel it throughout our entire being. This is passion. It is compelling emotion, eager interest and excitement.

Gathering inspiration from yourself and others is the key for a joyful life. When a person regularly reads, attends seminars, communicates with others and grows from life experiences, they have the chance to be inspired daily. When you do something and lose track of time, feel like it really isn't "work", or have that exhilarated rush while involved in an activity, you are following and using your passion. This is part of your full positive power.

ACTION AND ATTITUDE

The more wisdom, growth and knowledge you develop through reading, life experiences, learning from others, attending workshops, events, and seminars, the more you will grow. You then, in turn, help others by teaching and living by example. As a result of this, you glow with radiance and harmony naturally. What a wonderful way to live. Create your own opportunities and jump into them.

Many people plan and plan, set goals, dream and talk about what they want, without really doing. Others choose to have a bad attitude, blaming the economy, complaining about the people around them, and being moody. Neither of these ways is effective for moving forward in your life and exuding your true full positive power. You must want to improve your attitude, be aware of your thoughts, communication and language, and take steps of daily action toward what you want. This will add up to huge evolvement, improvements, opportunities and power.

SPIRIT AND SPUNK

When you meet a person with spunk, spirit or enthusiasm, you immediately feel drawn in. This is a contagious high energy, alertness and liveliness. It is a feeling of being full of life. When you are full of life, it is easier to feel not just happy, but fulfilled and satisfied with life. To gain more spirit and spunk, be around that type of people more often. Laugh more, don't take yourself so seriously, schedule in fun time, and make sure to do what you love every day - even just a little bit to start with. Think of some of the spirited, spunky people you know or know of. Now think of low energy, negative people. Who seems happier and more successful? Who seems more confident? Which do you want; spirited or mediocre, spunky or blah?

SAVVY

Being savvy is important to being in your full positive power and exuding confidence. To be savvy is to be clever and well informed. It is being able to decide ahead of time who is the right person to partner up with in your business; now and later down the road. It is being able to predict if the new business you create will succeed in your town; now and also in eight years. Being savvy gives you power, helps you to help others make decisions, and leads to great outcomes.

INTUITION, INTELLIGENCE AND IMAGINATION

Exuding your full positive power and confidence means to ask for help and information when you need it. Dare to ask for opportunities. Accepting help, kindness and generosity from friends and loved ones is an exceptional thing. It makes you feel loved and supported, and the other person feels great too. The important thing is to use this assistance as a growth experience. For example, if Mary is short on the rent by $500, and her best friend gives her money with no questions asked, Mary is secure for the month. Now that she is stable, she should use this opportunity to take steps toward earning the money herself for next month's rent, even saving some. However, if Mary expects her friend's generosity again the next month, her friend may begin to feel resentful. Instead, Mary can show her best friend appreciation by using that experience to get ahead.

It is great to receive, but when one ends up leaning on others too much by not coming up with their own decisions, steps and plans, they end up becoming co-dependent on others, which can lead to loss of their true self, confidence, inner purpose, and drive. The key is to accept generosity, learn and grow from it, and then give back by helping someone else. This will help you to have strong self-esteem, and the courage to move forward in your life. Powerfully ask how to get ahead, and learn from the people already doing it right.

TIPS AND TOOLS FOR ENHANCING INTUITION

1. Slow down, quiet the mind.
2. Be comfortable with the silence.
3. Focus on faint whispers of intuition or feelings.
4. Live in the moment.
5. Be receptive.
6. Remain aware and trust yourself.
7. Practice.

EXERCISE
IMAGINATION METHODOLOGY

The unfolding and evolvement of one's true self through exercises of intuition, visualization, writing, acting as if according to one's own psychological motives, personal identification and emotional state. The result is understanding and awareness of one's true self.

Imagine that it is three years from now, and there is an article in the paper listing you as the most influential or inspirational person in Southern California. Intuitively think of why this would be. Use your imagination to visualize.

Now take a few minutes to write down why you are that person. What have you done, how are you influencing or inspiring? What is your life like? Now, act it out. How would you feel? What would you say? This imprints it into your brain as a reality, making it more likely that it will truly occur.

EXERCISE

_____

_____

_____

_____

_____

_____

_____

_____

_____

_____

_____

_____

_____

_____

_____

_____

_____

_____

_____

_____

EXERCISE

OPEN-MINDED

Being open-minded = being powerful, kind and wise. You can truly learn from everyone you encounter. Maybe sometimes it's learning how you how don't want to be, but often you can gain insight from someone you run into at a random store, at your business, or at a networking event. Sometimes people believe that if they are an important CEO they cannot talk to the janitor, or vice versa. If you have no ego controlling the real you, you can appreciate and learn from everybody. Check on your beliefs, too. Be open-minded with your own should's and have-to's; turning them into want-to's.

NERVE

Make space for greatness. Life is about moving forward and always growing. Find, embrace and cherish your uniqueness. Let it out and appreciate it. Take a look at your life and answer the following questions to make sure you are moving forward. If a group of friends or colleagues wants you to go to an event with them, and you know they are generally negative and cause trouble, what do you do? Do you go out with them, knowing you'll go home feeling negative and drained, or do you choose to spend a quiet night at home with a glass of wine and a book? If you are at work and your client, patient, co-worker or boss talks to you very harshly, what do you do? Do you take offense, talk back, or have quiet strength? We have the choice to go down to the level of negative people, or to hold our heads high, knowing that being positive and our naturally happy selves is the right choice in the long run. When we continue to move forward in life, we move further away from negativity, and into the space of amazing, positive successful people.

Have the Nerve to be Yourself!

NOTES

_____

_____

_____

_____

_____

_____

_____

_____

_____

_____

_____

_____

_____

_____

_____

_____

_____

_____

_____

_____

_____

NOTES

_____

_____

_____

_____

_____

_____

_____

_____

_____

_____

_____

_____

_____

_____

_____

_____

_____

_____

_____

_____

_____

_____

_____

_____

NOTES

_____

_____

_____

_____

_____

_____

_____

_____

_____

_____

_____

_____

_____

_____

_____

_____

_____

_____

_____

_____

_____

NOTES

_____

_____

_____

_____

_____

_____

_____

_____

_____

_____

_____

_____

_____

_____

_____

_____

_____

_____

_____

_____

_____

_____

_____

_____

_____